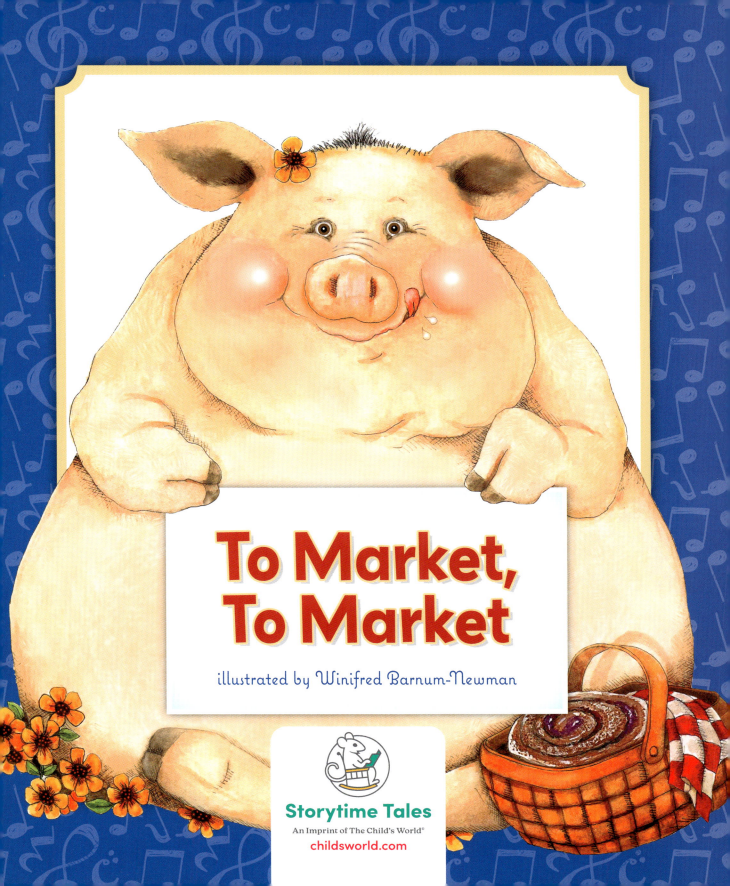

Published by The Child's World®
800-599-READ • www.childsworld.com

Copyright © 2023 by The Child's World®
All rights reserved. No part of this book may be reproduced or utilized in any form or by any means without written permission from the publisher.

Photography Credits
© mhatzapa/Shutterstock.com: design element; Beth Thompson/BethsNotesPlus.com: 3

ISBN Information
9781503865464 (Reinforced Library Binding)
9781503865792 (Portable Document Format)
9781503866638 (Online Multi-user eBook)
9781503867475 (Electronic Publication)

LCCN 2022939513

Printed in the United States of America

About the Illustrator

Winifred Barnum-Newman is an award-winning writer, poet, painter, sculptor, illustrator, and designer. She has also written newspaper articles. Winifred enjoys singing and playing the piano and guitar. She especially loves spending time with her children and grandchildren.

To Market, To Market

1. To mar-ket, to mar-ket to buy a fat pig. Home a-gain, home a-gain jig-ge-ty-jog.

2. To market, to market to buy a fat hog.
   Home again, home again, jiggety-jog.

3. To market, to market to buy a plum bun.
   Home again, home again, market is done.

To market, to market,
to buy a fat pig.

Home again, home again,

jiggety-jig.

To market, to market,
to buy a fat hog.

Home again, home again,

jiggety-jog.

To market, to market,
to buy a plum bun.

Home again, home again, market is done.

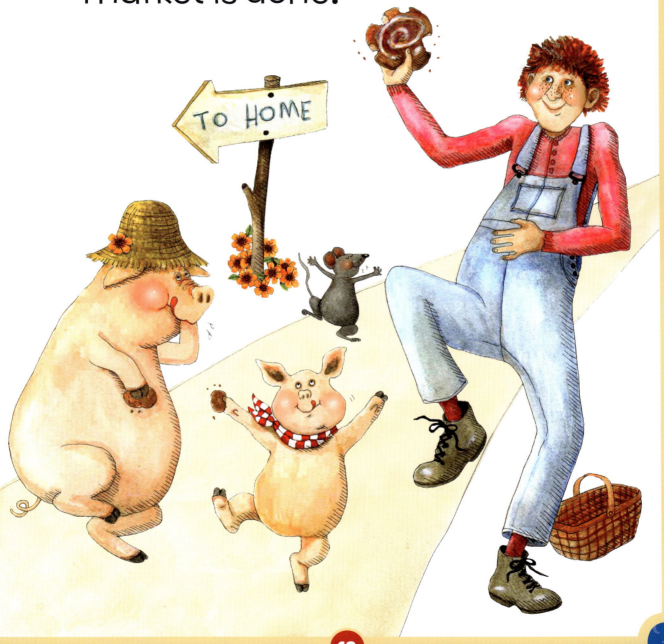

SONG ACTIVITY

Turn to your right and march in place.
Clap your hands four times
while marching when you say:
To market, to market, to buy a fat pig.

Face the front again and do a silly dance when you say:
Home again, home again, jiggety-jig.

Turn to your left and march in place.
Clap your hands four times
while marching when you say:
To market, to market, to buy a fat hog.

Face the front again and do an even sillier dance when you say:
Home again, home again, jiggety-jog.

Continue facing the front and march in place.
Rub your tummy in circles when you say:
To market, to market, to buy a plum bun.

Clap two times and take a bow when you say:
Home again, home again, market is done.

MORE ABOUT THIS SONG

This rhyming song is more than 400 years old. It tells the story of a person who buys a pig, then a hog. But what is the difference between the two animals? A pig is small and young. A hog is a fully grown pig that weighs more than 120 pounds (54 kilograms).

THINK ABOUT IT

Have you ever been to a farmers market? If so, what did you see? How is a farmers market different than a grocery store? Try to think of five ways the two are different. Write your answers on a piece of paper.

BENEFITS OF NURSERY RHYMES AND ACTIVITY SONGS

Activity songs and nursery rhymes are more than just a fun way to pass the time. They are a rich source of intellectual, emotional, and physical development for a young child. Here are some of their benefits:

- Learning the words and activities builds the child's self-confidence—"I can do it all by myself!"
- The repetitious movements build coordination and motor skills.
- The close physical interaction between adult and child reinforces both physical and emotional bonding.
- In a context of "fun," the child learns the art of listening in order to learn.
- Learning the words expands the child's vocabulary. He or she learns the names of objects and actions that are both familiar and new.
- Repeating the words helps develop the child's memory.
- Learning the words is an important step toward learning to read.
- Reciting the words gives the child a grasp of English grammar and how it works. This enhances the development of language skills.
- The rhythms and rhyming patterns sharpen listening skills and teach the child how poetry works. Eventually the child learns to put together his or her own simple rhyming words—"I made a poem!"